# To embrace growth

Nandini Verma

# To embrace growth

Nandini Verma

PAPER TOWNS
PUBLISHERS

PAPER TOWNS
PUBLISHERS

First published by
Papertowns Publishers
72, Vishwanath Dham Colony,
Niwaru Road, Jhotwara,
Jaipur, 302012

To Embrace Growth


ISBN Print Book – 978-93-94670-04-4



Cover by Neha Agrawal
nehaa.2089@gmail.com

# FOREWORD

Anne Frank said, "paper has more patience than people". This has been true across contexts and time periods. A poet is said to be the most aesthetic category of artists; though only if the poet enables its readers to construct an image out of his/her dark inked words.

The great Urdu poet Faiz Ahmed Faiz has repeatedly said that we shouldn't write for fashion and rewards, we must write what our heart says; or else don't write.

Crux being: don't feel shy/afraid to put your art out there, because if you are true to yourself then your art reflects this.

How should I convey my intangible feelings to you? Maybe just 'rhyme' them.

Observation is the key! If we are aware of what is happening around us, and we are able to express them in the easiest way possible, then that becomes art, because then it heals many souls in a righteous manner.

Poetry should define your soul, not your outward appearances!!

And, at last, the common misconception prevails; poets are sad by-default. So, to answer this, I must say that

Poets aren't necessarily sad, they just feel more.

**Sahil Gera,**
**Author of the book "sukhan"**

# CHAPTERS:

1. Querencia
   {a place from which one's strength is drawn, where one feels at home; the place where you are your most authentic self}

2. Agapity
   {the highest form of love; selfless, sacrificial, and unconditional love; persists no matter the circumstance}

# Artistic vantage:

It's nothing unusual what artists see,
It's just how they see it
Coalesce of analogies, as though it were two worlds; two planets
They're liberal, within themselves whilst perceiving ideas and feelings
Those perceptions aren't impractical or imaginative
Abstract? Yes
How long could you drown in reality anyways
Artists are liberal while they are discerning the immortalised living abstractness between the chemistry of the air
Like inspiration, beauty and it's kinfolks.
Creativity is not a skill, it's an undulated habit
It can't be possessed
and you can't own creativity
A human body is far too miniscule to accumulate the vastness of the abstractism that creativity comes along with
It's an undulated habit in a way that a mere person can only chase to acquire and lay it out in their work.
And no artist is perfect in being creative
That itself is the agility of creativity to slip out of people's hands
Even those who wish to grab it and squeeze it in their works
An artist's vantage is merely close to perfection

It's vast
It's everything with a little bit of creativity.

# My mother

My mother is a prestigious figure
She has not only succeeded in following the socially assigned and limitless principles
but also done it with sheer kindness
She has paid her price for being a tolerant woman
and she has done it with kindness
Her light brown eyes are comforting despite the tears that have rushed out of them.
She has spent a huge fraction of her life making someone else's worthwhile
and she has done it with kindness
She's lived those mundane routine days for more than over two decades so that someone's bread isn't burnt
and she has done it with kindness
But I have seen the prodigious beast underneath her silk saree and selfless smiles.
How it roars with the will to break free
but she has made the society happy by living up to their meaning of motherhood
And she has done it with kindness

# Nurture

In the evening of an afterbirth of a catastrophe,
I tried to elucidate my upset mind
I tried to translate the crumbling of my heart.
It didn't require algorithms but it wasn't simple either.
The tears wanted to be an accessory
They wanted to be seen, they did not want to be heard
They did not want to be consoled or shooed away
Just an easy escape is what they demand
And maybe the sunflowers in me found no sun
And maybe those songs that I wrote belonged to the trash can
The pain was, and is still ineradicable.
But the sunflowers can now bloom
The songs still crawl up to the frets and strings of my guitar
There is pain, progress and primacy for myself.

## Hobbies

Maybe I like myself
I like the way I swing my arms in the spring of my heart
Or how I suddenly become so beautiful
When the summer waters hush walks past my earlobes
I don't like those skies empty
So I find my acrylics and fill my sky
I paint it crimson and blue
And then a paper and a pen is just not enough
To fathom all the chaos in me
That's when the strokes on my canvas play
That's when my voice on my guitar becomes bolder
than before.
That's when I'm channelising my countless expressions
in infinite ways.

# Minimal Overflow

It takes an excessive amount of courage to absorb the
fact that your life is in your hands, yet not give up on it.
It's a huge responsibility for merely a moving cluster of
forever in service, unintegrated, compartmentalised,
robotic organs
Humans spend most of their lives by either granting
themselves of what they want or with contrition of what
they couldn't
But no one appreciates courage within themselves.
'Courage' the beautiful yet impious feeling.
The courage you use to keep going, that means so much
to your family.
You can achieve courage
Just not by the hollow unfairly used courage spent on
individual holism in theocracies.
It's not God that helps
It's not his unpopular ways to communicate back with
you
But courage that keeps you going
That makes you do something worthwhile with your life
And if you ever need hope
You don't have to look at the sky
And ask for renting a little house up there
But turn your back at your older self
See how far you've come, even if you have just started.
And I promise you
That

Is going to make you more courageous than God ever could.

# Being brave

Being brave,
Isn't even climbing mountains all by yourselves
For me,
It's just the uncompromisable will to live each day.
And if you're doing that
You're appreciated

# How to open a body

At eight,
All a normal soul could ever know
Was nothing.
But at that age if she pities her skin, her body parts
Then she's much more than just
an eight year old girl
She's a black hole
Containing all that she has heard of herself
All that she has been through.
If one night,
Her unlucrative body is ripped open
Without her knowledge of what those body parts were
capable of,
Then she's hungry too
Of giving voice to the old her
Who was not to speak a word about
how she was vilely cut open.
She's much more than words and actions.
She might be all flustered about the pain in her orifices.
About how it could give lives to the unborn.
And then if she grew into elegance and grace
With such episodes swallowing her moments in the
present
Then she's much more than just a woman with a
purpose
There's a lot for her.
A lot of her share is left

Of happiness and love.

# Ignominy

I know myself,
A little.
I have blemishes in my temperament
In my personality
But I have capabilities too
That might not show on my skin
All they want to do is
Test my perfection
Knowing I am not.
They know
somewhere I am scarred
And they'll use my scars to tell the world
That I am made of flaws.
Of how flaws were intentionally chosen by me
They'll tell the world I have too much skin,
Or too much bone
Or too much muscle.
Where all those things have hidden in it a greater suffering
Than just cuts and wounds
That has sustained a growing will to end myself.
So it doesn't matter to me
If my scars don't please you
It doesn't matter to me
That I trusted you and you showed everyone what my outside is

It doesn't matter to me if a couple hundred people saw
my bodily flaws
Before they knew my journey.
My bad reputation is just your impatient judgement
Not the fault in my scars.

# Insecurities

I look at the others
And then I look at myself
Curse myself to tears,
For what I look like.
But when I look at myself
And then turn to others
I praise myself
For what I am.
I reminisce and respect the episodes from my journey in being.
And then no one makes me feel small or scant.
So prioritise and respect it
Turn your truck loads of love
That you so selflessly give to others
to yourself
And that will make you thrive
In ways you always wanted to
Respect your journey in being
And it will make you so comfortable in your skin.
So look at others, admire them
But save the love for yourself.

# Roots

The feeling of belongingness
Is the most beautiful one.
The feeling of knowing you belong
To a set of people, to a place, to a culture
How we turn to our home
When the day gone
Has been miserable.
We've always had a place to be in.
To be for.
More than just cemented walls,
There are perfect pillows to cry on
Perfect shower to wash the misery in
Perfect food to fuel ourselves
Perfect pens to make our future live,
Perfect family to be in.
So don't fall apart
Once you're all by yourself
Just because you're a few kilometres away
Does not mean you don't belong to where you came from
Let your new life take its time
To germinate the freshness of the living
Till then keep your roots
alive, watered and flourishing.
Always.

# ‘No’

How will I balance my YESes when I’m not allowed to say NO?

# Uncovered shoulders

My uncovered shoulders don't expect attention from
hungry men.
But now that it's such a big deal.
I have started asserting restrictions on myself
I've started telling my shoulders
'no, you don't belong in the comfort of people's eyes'
They have been verbally assaulted by myself
So now they droop a little more everyday I grow
As a woman.
And the safest I can look is
In shapeless clothes
Where my feminine figure is least shown.
Where I am less likely to be a victim to the hungry men
Little do I wish
It was comfortable to people that I wore my sundress
outside my bathroom.
Where I could openly look feminine.
Where I didn't have to hide my concavity.
But I choose not to fight the billion hungry men.
For it has now become easier for me
To not wear what I want to
But to fight for my uncovered shoulders.

## Inexperienced

In the process of imparting my pieces
From my secret diary to this book
It has taken a cosmic quantity of courage.
Maybe it's a part of growing up, it's a part of letting go.
So now I'm leaving my expressions to be consumed by vulnerability.
By people's opinions on my way of thinking.
But if I'm strong enough
To open
A little window to the heart in my brain,
If I'm strong enough to pierce through
a sword of criticism that I have never liked,
Then I guess I can take it.
I can take the need to sink the madness in.
The anger,
Not because they would criticise,
But because I haven't given them the right to.
There's very little that can awaken the sleeping storm in me
My story that has never been told.
The pain evident in the weaving of my sentences
And everything that comes along with expressing.
So there's a long way my courage has to come
In this journey
For writing a book,
Is not just 'writing a book'
It's much more than that.

It's awakening the storm, the untold reasons for my abysmal behaviour and the bravely woven sentences.
It's much more than trying to comfort
First, me
And then the others who are too bullied by their emotions.
It's much more than finding oneself.
Writing a book is providing help
To anyone and everyone who needs it.
Who's in search of something specific.
So here I am
Exercising courage at every word that you read.
Because writing a book is much more
than writing a book.

# Complexion

As a little child,
I played in the sun
Till the sun went down the horizon
And everyday I asked my parents,
Why I was so tinted
I asked them,
If it made me look ugly
They told me
That I still looked like the princess of their dreams
But that didn't ever make me not discover
Scrubs and ways to turn fair
Where eight years after,
Now I wear this tan affectionately
Knowing I symbolise my land.
Knowing I represent the brownness
Of where I belong
So why do I have to turn to anything
I am not meant to turn into
When the brownness chose me

# Blue

Blue has been my choice
Even before I realised
That as a little girl
I always fell under baby pink.
Blue was for my brothers,
My male counterparts.
Who were never expected to be soft or sensitive,
They had to keep the masculinity of the colour going.
Even if it meant that they had to suppress their tears
within
The boundaries of their eyes.
Even if it meant that they could feel angry, but not hurt.
They were supposed to be strong or they would have
been less men.
And I solely believe that it's not only injustice to their
feelings
But to their right to feel a particular way.
When did we become so biassed about how a gender is
assigned to feel?
When did we decide that "boys don't cry"?
When did we decide that as tots, boys looked like boys
in blue.

# Lost Womanhood(Talibani women)

On behalf of all those
Who never learnt enough words
To be verbally,
Even socially valid.
Who are not given attention
Only because they don't know how much the sympathy can comfort them
Women have fled lands, with their babies.
Raised trauma and frustration into strength and privilege.
So who gave you the right to manipulate anatomy granted to everyone?
That a woman's existence would be the genesis of all criminality?
That liberty does not exist in women's wardrobes?
Matriarchal subjugation is all that will live
Even if one day they wipe out the female population.
I pity this world who hasn't seen the pretty faces
Under black burqas.
I pity this world who has left so many capabilities to the confined spaces in the dark.
I pity the new born girl child who will never be able to imagine that for all her lifetime she will never be seen
Her adventurous heart will give up by the age of nine.
I pity this world which has not let half of its population grow in their own capacities.

I pity this world who hasn't let women learn enough words
To tell the world how much she can achieve,
How much she can be.

## How to count on what you have not lost.

There was an evening
After I lost a friend
And it wasn't just me who did,
It was the whole body, that lost
Balance, when we lost a friend.
That evening,
All of us fifteen year olds
Heartbroken,
Put our arms around each other and
Stood in a huge circle,
Looked up, and there
Fell tears on the ground
Like rain for the ants.
But at that moment,
No rivalries or fights mattered to anyone,
And we probably forgot
What we meant to each other.
All we knew,
And all we felt,
Was how much we mean to the friend
Who wasn't with us.
Who was a happy little mitochondria
Who never wanted to stop growing.
But he did,
He would have been battling himself
Just to breathe longer,
To stay,

To discover the undiscovered in his bucket list.
To laugh with his friends,
To study,
To play,
To become someone.
But he couldn't make it that far.
But today it's not about
What he couldn't do
It's about what he did,
He lived in every moment
With excellent vigour
He made sure no one was having a bad day.
He was capable of achieving what he dreamt of,
And that's what made him live big.
I'm still sorry for what we lost,
But he's not going anywhere,
From the durable organ we call 'heart'.
And in that moment,
I learnt
What it can cost
For taking everything, every moment for granted.
In that moment
I lost the most I could,
As a fifteen year old child
But I secured a massive amount of respect
For what I hadn't.
So, one day
If your friend walks up to you
And yells at you
For telling their secrets to someone else,

Shut them up, hug them
And tell them that it's great to see them
Healthy and alive.

## Dark circles

They feed on the feelings I don't want to nurture.
But I can't ever call them less beautiful
Because they symbolise pain.

# Control

They can't tell me
How to control my emotions
I have done it in moments,
When it's hardest to.
I've kept the pain beating in my chest
Like someone stuck a cane in the juncture
of where my lungs meet.
I've pressed my sobs behind my vocal cord.
I've comforted the restless beast in me,
that could destroy a world or two
I have tamed my tears well
And that's enough control for me.

# Teenagery

To build on the will to fly
You must be caged once.
Caged with liberties
We're only getting warmed up
To set fire to our dreams.

## Less valued

You always came as one body
And you will leave it as one
So why cling on to people to
feel less lonely?
When the parts of you want them to be valued by you.
When the undiscovered atoms in your body
Want to find a place
Find a job
in making you successful
In making you whole.
So don't go crazy
Trying to find someone
Who would want a place in your heart
When so much of you had already been waiting
To be a valued part of you.

# Endurance

What a brave human being you are
For single-handedly steering your life
All along the ugly turns
Of the indecisive world.
When all of the universe
Was choosing the more convenient way
To win their ambition,
You stuck by the toilsome road
Where at every turn
There was a bigger sacrifice to make
Where you're all alone
Working day and night.
Far apart from the entertainment,
What a beautiful human being you are,
For being so dedicated to your future self.

# Speechless

It's nothing but a little hiccup
When my words run out of my heart
When they feel shaky to let it dodge through the twists of my tongue
So I let it reroute to my eyes;
On my skin, where the goosebumps don't demand control.
It's a little moment
Of nothingness in my voice
Yet expression in all of my body.

# Painless

I don't feel pain when I'm in pain.
I feel like a wilted sunflower
Rooted on the edge of Neptune.
I feel like the hopeless niceness of tragedies.

## Ever since yesterday

Yesterday,
I blushed when I looked at myself
In the mirror,
When I looked at my imperfections I did not cry.
Yesterday, I swore to my shiny brown hair
That I will open them in the wind of racing cars.
Yesterday, I taught my lips how to smile.
Yesterday I looked into my own wet eyes and wiped off the little flood that was in it.
Yesterday I promised my skin that I will moisturise it with so much sunshine
That my heart that I'll fill with gold, gets all jealous
Ever since yesterday, I have wanted to look as tall as I am.
As curvy as I am.
Yesterday, I changed
And ever since yesterday,
I have finally started loving
every
little
bit
of me.

# School

It has taught me,
That everyday
No matter how badly you fail
You're always going to have to
Polish your shoes, do your homework
And show up like a winner.

# Coexisting with the dead

The thought of 'dying'
Isn't as dark and depressing as it appears to be.
At least for me

At least for me,
It blooms a thousand flowers inside
For I only want to be with
Those people
With warm bedrooms on the stars.

# Moving skies

I am as blue as the sky was,
Today
The sky was my help,
It was my escape.
I lay on the grass
My eyes filled with the hues of blue
Blinded to the horizon
And for the first time in my life so far,
I felt at home
For once,
I felt welcomed
For once there was nothing more that I needed
Than something not human
To understand me so completely.

# Emptiness

If there is so much space in the vastness
Of this universe,
Then why couldn't people have bigger hearts?

# When a poem ends

Sometimes when I'm reading poetry
And read a poem end
I wish for it's continuation in my head
For a thought never suddenly
goes off to sleep.
It just fades away to the subconscious of the poet
And probably never ever returns to
Validation.
But how I wish
I could openly be a part of the thought so beautiful
Someone felt, and then put it in my head.
Sometimes I wish that no poetry should never end

# Recovery everyday

For me
The sky doesn't darken
Because of the solar mood swings
I think
The skies keep on
Gulping from my share of
Toxicity
And turns dark blue
In the most beautiful way,
cosmically shouts
And tells me
That there's another tomorrow.

# Poems are literary nomads

Sometimes
I feel a poem piercing through the mundane thoughts
of everydays
And rushing out of my head.
So before it is all scattered and dispersed in the air,
I unfold it on a paper
Before I lose it.
But sometimes, I have also felt a poem
Coming along a person
And staying in my head for years.
Sometimes, a poem comes to me
When I'm ready for it
But sometimes,
It comes at moments where I can't grab it as proof
Of being home to beautiful nomadic expressions.
Sometimes, I am so glad I can feel the poems coming
But sometimes I get jealous
Of people who existed before I was even born
and used the beautiful expressions
That I feel now
I find poems unexpectedly.
Yet in the best ways.

## Dear heart

In this lifetime,
I hope we find healing
Like balm on chapped lips
I hope we find infinite ways
To fall in love with each other.

## Simpler things

Come;
To the unwalked trails
Of the park of nothingness
Let's soak the dew drops of the fresh grass
To our bare feet.
Try to become a more important consumption of space
While we unknowingly battle
While we unknowingly win.
Let's not try to fit in
Into this endless horizon
Or hide ourselves in the
Dingy dungeons of our timidity.
Who are we?
But fools
Trying to make our life perfect.

# Mundanity

I am passionate about writing
Yet so often
I am a poemless nomad
In the air of mundanity.
Trying to figure out
How I'm blocking ideas,
But then it isn't that evil
For it lets me be
In the practicalities that I dislike.
It's necessary to know
That life isn't always
In love songs and orchids.

# Woven

I feel as though
I need to pick up the needle of realisations,
Attach it to the thread of acceptance
and stitch the cuts
opened up by people in my past.
I need to weave the cuts in beautiful patterns,
So that the ugliness that my body carries is concealed
till the next person
I am going to love
rips it open again.

# Nightmare #46

I was on fire, looking in the direction of the endless sky.
And there he was waiting for me, with his arms wide
open, whispering, 'Just let go'
Slowly I was evaporating as ashes of my own
And we were living the life we always dreamt of,
The childish fantasies of living on clouds.

# I write

I write
Yes I write
For the words slip off my tongue wrongly,
And then alphabets hold hands
Grip on my fingers
And the unsaid is left unsaid.

# 3:00 a.m. sky

The sky feels different
At 3:00 a.m.
It feels as though the stars are ready
To fall
Like autumn leaves

# I hate to hurt

I hate that I cannot fight back for myself on the spot.
I hate that it bothers me until
I finally come with the one sentence
That could hurt my enemy.
And I hate that I don't want to hurt
The people who hurt me.
I hate that my impulsive decisions
Are incapable
To tell them
That there's a fierce poet
Verbally successful.
Who is not bold enough,
To use it to scar the relationships.
I hate that I am a part of the quiet and ignorant
population
Of this raging world.

# Hug

I don't know who to ask from
When I feel the need to
Put my arms around
a cylindrical figure
With shoulders and a heartbeat.
When I have the urge
to feel weak and untouched,
while I am wrapped around the figure.
Where for once,
I can leave myself and
Timidly
Hold onto the loving cylindrical figure
And expect to have the right
To hold onto it forever.

# Unwanted flower

I might be the
Unwanted wilted flower,
the gardener coldly plucks,
but then he
Crushes me and puts me
In the manure
So that the other flowers
That deserved to live - grow.

# BINGO

I haven't been loved
By someone more selfless
Than the four legged creature,
That has a voice but only to express that it's overwhelmed.
Who doesn't mind hour long hugs
And is covered with loyal fur.
I feel ashamed for I can write
About someone who left me
For no reason,
But I can't write endlessly about my dog
Who's been living and loving beautifully
Amongst species that are
Not even of its own.

# I'm so full, yet not enough

When I'm writing
I feel as though
I am imparting molecules verbally.
I feel as though
I am shedding
The weight of beautifully heavy
Expressions
So that I only have to bother about
Keeping its grace once,
While decorating it with
Analogies alike.
So that I don't have to
Carry its delight
Into the days where I fall on my knees and cry,
For not being enough.

# Leaving Home

I left home
at the age of twelve,
thinking that it is
going to be
as comforting as my mother's lap,
but I got to the dormitory,
And for a year,
all I could feel was lonesome.
My parents when they saw their daughter's swollen eyes,
Brokedown each time.
And I hated telephones and emails,
For it only convinced me that they're far.
I would get scared each night
for the bed on the top
had no arms like my father's
to put my hair away so that I could get good sleep every night.
I would sit on my windowsill
For hours,
Hoping I'll see my family come through,
and take me back to the place,
I was never ready to leave.

# Bandages

I think bandages,
Are the most beautiful invention
I have them all over,
Sometimes on my skin
Sometimes on the wounds inside.
I have it on every repaired piece of me.
I have drawn inspiration from a thing as simple as a bandage.
And I'm so grateful that bandages and I exist in the same universe.
I'm so grateful that something without feelings can heal so much better.

# Paradise

Don't make me leave so early,
I haven't lived enough in this paradise.

## Wounds as though mulberries

I have been told I'm beautiful,
But you convinced me
That my bruises resembled mulberries,
That embraced itself
As a fruit
Of your existence.

# The 'normal' undreamt of

While I traverse
Across the city,
In fine dresses
And big cars,
With phones and wallets,
I traverse,
Relieved of the fact that
I am going back to a place
Never out of food,
Or warmth or love.
But I see so many infants,
Wounded, begging and glowless
Hanging horribly
On one side of their caretaker.
I see men with
Bone shivering deformities,
Carrying it along
Their imperfect and
Unheard voices.
They walk from one end of the city
To another.
Working for a ten-rupee note that would
Show them their way to hope
Struggling for a little place that's more than plastic sheets and wasted food.
The sole of my feet hasn't touched the streets,
And theirs is as though made of it.

When one gets to know,
That little babies have seen
More struggle than one's adult self
It breaks my belief
In empathy.
I hope the unlucky set of people in this world,
Someday find the courage
To dream of sleeping on a bed.

# Deterioration

Why is it that,
All beauty is only analogous with nature?
Are humans so mal-hearted that they couldn't
Put hands to something that would sustain
Purity?

# The ache

It's been a few months
Of constant cramps in my soul.
In my world, the sun has stopped rising.
And I could not even gather
The little energy I thought you left in me,
To face it and ask why.
The heartache got me bed ridden for months,
And I don't know for how long I'll continue
Fearing the simple idea of meeting someone
Who'll cause me so much pain
So much ache.

# Strength

There's a whole lot of pain
Under my lashes.
A lot of progress left
to see me do

# Apocalypse (corruption)

There's an apocalypse,
growing in it's frequencies,
Somewhere,
feeding on the loud muffled noises of sins,
And it'll exist
till humanity in my journey
turns
to dust .

## Cosmic aggression

The day you left,
The sun in my world died.

# Wind of contentment

The wind of contentment,
Gave birth to the breeze
That caresses my problems,
The air that whistles
And blows my hair away,
So that it can whisper in my ear.
It's not a tornado today,
It's the wind of contentment.

# Soul

A few months ago,
I was losing faith in the voice
That held my soul together.
But I let it hold me,
Even though there was resistance.
However now,
I'm grateful to myself
For walking me to that point in time
Where I am so content
Wearing myself on my soul.

# Prison

It's dimly lit,
The chambers of my heart,
Where the prisoners live.
Who have been plunged in affection and fruit.
Yet they cried for freedom and tasted humanity.
The prisoners
Have become so covetous,
After having lived on the golden of my body,
After walking on the cushion of
Thick experiences.
Who have always been
Suffering fulfilment.
They are prisoners
Of niceness beyond humanity
They are prisoners to love
Love from me.

# Overfed

I am overfed with heartbreaks.

# Entangled earphones

It's a different kind of ache
When I see my earphones entangled,
But then it also fiddles with my hopelessness
And reaches the ears of my shut heart
Tells me that even the thing which carries me to absolute solace,
Doesn't exist uncomplicatedly
Withholds the rage with mess of its own,
Of carrying the solace so conveniently to my ears.
My entangled earphones pinch my deteriorated soul,
While they're plugged in,
And force me to not break the flow of
Softly carrying the divine mix of
songs you and I revered for our little relationship that it barely became.
It forces me to listen to us almost crossing lines to reach detected love.
My entangled earphones are suffering from a whole other type of hurt.
But in its simplicity, it adorns my time, most of my day.
Implicitly, my earphones are the transport to a world I made for us.

# "Big girl"

I can't remember what it was like
To be mumma's big girl,
When my hands were as big as paper boats
That tirelessly held on to dreams
Of an unbelievably nice world.
When my feet never fit
One tenth of my father's combat boots,
But they walked on excellence in
Reaching the top of the fridge
Or winning a poem recitation.
Now I excel in,
Living through sun-less days
Without breaking down
Or writing a thousand poems in secrecy
About how I want to end everything.
I can't remember being a naive nomad.

# Cracked

Loneliness is a lot more
Than finding company in the cracks
Of the wall your bed is glued to.
The way I start crying
When I see cracks just anywhere
And feel as though you have caused it
Everywhere.
Because once upon a time
The world was home to me
And now it's cracked
Open into pitch darkness.
Now you're in my former home
Punching it, to expand.
Finding love, living in perfect trance.
But the punching is causing several other crack-births in my world.
Till it shrinks till it only fits my heart
And then you'll happily crack that too.

# Failure

My efforts walk through disfigurement
After failure smashes on my face
And the shattering convinces me
That I am nothing
But a planted space
For tolerating incoherence
And infused atrocities
Of this world that
Works like an unending jigsaw
You fit in or you don't
I currently reside in grey walls and dim lights
With aching retinas and an exhausted spine
Retaliation to betrayal
Punches me back
With developed fists
So, I rebuild myself
Into an unapologetic being, and
I try it differently each time.
So manipulate me into my numb corner of
Failure and dust.
Where isolation welcomes me with open arms and
consumes me completely.

# The Clock on my Heart

I had been haunted
By how fast time flew.
It would cause me ugly anxiety,
Especially at night
When another day awaited
So that I could mince my plans.
The day I found you though
I wore time,
Underneath my kind skin
And spun the clocks
Till I reached a moment
Where for the minutest second you were falling in love with me.

# Pursuit

If Poetry or Art
Was a person,
I would become that lover,
The world thinks
Only exists in fiction.

# Empowerment

I sit with the elder men in my family
Contribute to the discussions on finance and business.
Even though I am just a curious
Seventeen year old girl

But I don't overlook the movements
In the dusty corner of the smoky kitchen
Where the elder women of my family toil.

I am here,
Sipping from the expensive bone china.
They are cleaning the spilled tea from
The hands of the nervous girl,
Who boldly convinces everyone her
Place in the overcrowded yet little
Room of empowered women.

I have been born in the era
Where knowledge has been defeated by
Age and gender..

How I wish I could convince my mother
The day she was getting married
To never give up on accentuating
Empowerment in her life
Till she becomes a person that can,
At least put herself above others.

But seeing her work in a confined
Space that has chimneys full of frustration
I realise,
That what she has done is not less
What she has sacrificed is not less.

Only if I could see her wearing a crown,
Walking in a gown shimmering of confidence
Since she would have bought it on her own

I could never love anything in this world,
I could never want to become anything else,
But the more empowered and independent version
Of my mother.

# Realising i have been hurt

There is an unwanted winter in my rhapsodies,
When feelings meet freedom.
Or are those battles between them?
Is this pain real?
Have I really experienced
My skin tearing apart
While the tornados of bad luck
Settle on me,
Raging.
Have I really struggled to watch the sun
From my unmade bed
In the absence of lights that were
Last switched on,
Day before yesterday.
Or is it just my terrifying capacity
To create emotional monsters?
Or just this annoying trait in me
To let my emotions rule?
Now,
I just witnessed my yesterdays melting into today,
So softly,
So smoothly.
I am unaware of the reality that calls me.
All I seem to know if of the cold
Worsening in the nerves
That verbalise the snowstorms in my soul.

# Bury my heart

I walked into myself
To find warmth
That i couldn't feel
Since I was so invested in fighting the
Limitations of mortal minds.
I walked into myself,
Expecting a part of me to
Welcome my conscious.
Instead I walked till I found my heart frozen
from the cold that I let into it.
I could have postponed my own death
For heaven's sake.
But my innocence;
My innocence let me ask for taking the fall
For a failed attempt to find love,
My heart rests,
In complete numbness
I don't know - dead or alive
Frozen to the core.
But now at least I don't have to worry about letting pain
get to the dead.
So bury my heart
Or return all the love I so selflessly gave away
Return all that love
To put a beat in my heart.

# I left a long time ago

Even my eyes,
Expressed the requirement to come out
As they bulged out
Swollen, red and wet.
Like my soul,
When it pushed the wall beneath my skin,
Somewhere near my chest
Where it hurt the most
So now,
if , even the organs in my body
And the life in my body wants to leave
How am I supposed to suppress it?
I am with them,
I am them.
I want to leave too .

## Agapity

{the highest form of love; selfless, sacrificial, and unconditional love; persists no matter the circumstance}

# You Chapter

Here's the chapter,
I promised you.
Here's the chapter only to tell you
That I include you
in understanding art.

# Little box 'love'

Under the warm sun of April
In a global crisis,
I found all that I needed to complete
My voids in the broken little box I call 'love'.
I found a handsome collection of molecules.
Who knew, when we first met,
That I'll long to be held in his athleticism.
That I'll long to be an inhabitant in his chivalric heart.
But once I did, it became a million battles tougher,
For I underestimated the patience I had
To wait for what he once promised I'll have.
I want to fill my voids with solitarily- you.
So let my fragmentarity be,
If you're never coming back.
I'm not letting the wrong person mis-match the patches of my box
For the sake of making it look like it's fixed.
The little box I call 'love'.

# I wish I could

Hold my heart,
Caress it,
Fix it with glue
Feed it self- love
And then silently put it in its food
A tranquilliser
That could forever numb it's pounding so intense
I wish I could
Silently kill it's will to grow
Kill it's will to solicit love
I wish I could though
I really wish I could
But then I see your face
And then disdain all the pain in my heart
At that moment,
Where your eyes meet mine
I disregard the hurting
I feel complete
And then I wish I had a heart
In my heart
I really wish.

# Hopeless Attachments

I'm attached to him
As much as I am to my organs.
I am attached to him
As much as the earth is to the sun
Like the sun has bigger businesses to take care of
But the earth lives in its presence.
Walking into the entanglement of the strings that I have amalgamated to him,
I didn't realise the mess I put myself in, I just kept praising where I was.
But when he finds time and looks into himself,
Maybe he'll help me
Help me escape my hopeless attachments.
Cut all my strings,
Or maybe I'll keep walking until he throws me far away
To never find a way back
Into what I once called home
which once I felt safe
Attaching myself to.

## Presence

Presence is beautiful
Especially when you are more than just aware ,
When your whole body thanks you
For making it happen
For being close to that one person
Because that's how much it matters to me.
Being next to you
Knowing you're alive
Knowing I can touch you
For being able to expect a response.
My body thanks me for
Choosing someone who won't give up so easy
On their life.
Because in the past,
I have lost someone so close that makes me fade
everyday
So now I go along hand in hand with time
Thanking it for what it's letting me experience
The good and the simple.
I miss what's unreachable in the sky
Who was supposed to be here,
With me.
Who promised that we'll always be together
Who carried me along all his uncertainties.
Left me crushed
And hurting.
Battling all I could think of and what I could not.

The massive wish to be in his presence
That I could not have anymore.
So here I am.
Anxious yet grateful
To see what war
Time makes me fight ahead.

# Selfishness

You're not looking for people
When you're looking for people
You're just looking for qualities that will comfort you.
You're not looking for love
After reading romantics
You're just desperate to be loved.
So don't say you're not selfish,
When it comes to loving.
Don't declare your claim on my respected heart.
If we have to,
We'll find the selfless in each other
And then never fall apart.
Don't tell me that you don't expect for only
Gold dripping down my ribcage.
So that you can tell everyone
You own someone expensive.
Someone not easy to love.
Don't tell me that you would accept my imperfections,
Because when you saw a glimpse of it
It made you leave me in the middle of our beginning.
don't tell me you're not selfish,
When you snatch the selflessness that I direct to you.

# Mountains

Mountains are massive
Massive enough to bother about all our extravaganza.
The world has made us crave peace at seventeen.
So let us walk together,
On the uneven terrain of open mountain valleys
Where the light sun and no human voices are.
Let us hold hands
And be viewers
To the verdancy of the heights, nature let us make a home on.
Let us watch
The furry animals and the gushing river.
The clouds would be kissing the snow till it melts.
And so would you to me
And the mountains would all hold hands
Accommodate us in a little cottage in its vastness.
There wouldn't be screens or people to care for.
Just you and I
Our home.
And our mountains.

# Eyes

We're over,
But whenever I watch you
Do absolutely anything,
Whenever I get the mere glimpse of your simple existence,
I try to promise myself
To look away
To not plunge myself into the gleam of your eyes.
My eyes drown themselves in their own rain,
While I watch yours, watch mine.
And your eyes become the voiceless billion fantasies
That I wish I could be a part of.
Your eyes become the fire, I'd like to be kept warm in.
The parts of your eyes try to tell mine to leave,
But have you ever looked into mine,
Try to swim across the floods to save me from drowning
So, now left all alone,
For choosingly all my life,
I will learn how to swim while I drown.
For you will never turn back and watch me
With your mahogany eyes.
And I'll never be able to see the world
Through the reflections in your eyes.
I'll never be able to see myself smiling,
Through your eyes.

# Unkind sources of Love

Why make someone so hopeful
About 'unbreakable bonds'
When you yourself fail to
practice your part of it?
One-way bonds have no confluence
They go on hopelessly forever.
So why would you make me waste
All of my passion
On something so unachievable.
Something that doesn't matter
To someone who matters to me the most.
What do you call this
Sweet misleading?
Because that's where your 'I love you' came from.

## Endurance

What a brave human being you are
For single-handedly steering your life
All along the ugly turns
Of the indecisive world.
When all of the universe
Was choosing the more convenient way
To win their ambition,
You stuck by the toilsome road
Where at every turn
There was a bigger sacrifice to make
Where you're all alone
Working day and night.
Far apart from the entertainment,
What a beautiful human being you are,
For being so dedicated to your future self.

# Come back

Everytime I write about you
To the best of my ability,
I can't help but use words like 'billions and millions and endless and always'
Everytime I try to remember how your touch felt on my skin
I can't help but feel the adrenaline washing over like waves of an ocean in the stormy night.
Everytime I look at you, not needing me
I can't help but close my eyes as though I wanted to turn blind.
Come back, for my blood is frozen in all those parts you haven't touched me in.
Come back, for I can take what you come with, I can nurture what you have.
Come back, for I need to feel my body against your skin,
Come back, because I cry on every word I write about your absence in my life,
Come back for the way we parted wasn't right
Come back for my hands are only yours to be held
Come back for my lips have dried saying your name
And I will abandon all that you hate about me
I'm ready to face the endlessness of life's expectations.
Only if you come back
So to the one who I am in love with so vehemently,
Please come back.

## Unregretful

You watch her like you have
A thousand stories to catch up on
Like how I'll like being looked at,
But I don't really think
Any of us will be alive
Once you're
ready to be mine.

## How I fall in love with you

I fall in love with you all over again
With every renewing thought of you.
I fall in love with you as fresh as
Pink dandelions in my garden
I fall in love with you so intense
Each time I think of us walking under the warm sun
On the grassland of our favourite mountains.
I fall in love with you with my arms extended to all the ends
Of your existence.
I fall in love with the way you touch me
And run your hands over my skin
I fall in love with myself in your eyes
I fall in love with the way you win me everyday.
I fall in love with you all over again
Every living second of my life.

# Irony

It's so ironic
They way I told you that
love - ceased to ever exist in my life
About how hopeless the four lettered word had gotten for me,
And then falling in love
So intensely with you
That now I have forgotten for second time
What it would be like
To be loved again.

# A second time

Seated across my windowsill
Looking at the skies
That hold our history
I realise
That just assemblance of words
Is not all that I have to do
To ever win you back.
I realise that
Using the poetry from my deepest dungeons
That you have been a visitor to
Is just not enough
To have you love me like you did.
Is it that impossible?
To have us back
Something so pure and divine.
Was it such a heavy load to carry
Something that once made you feel so light
Is it really so hard to
Love someone again, you were ready to love
For an entire lifetime.
Am I so upsetting
That having me love you
With all the bravery with which I could,
Set you so far apart?
You promised us a second chance
After the sky is washed
And I'm preparing myself

Everyday for either
loving you so perfectly
That you'd thank me for
Keeping the sky hold onto us
For a little longer.
Or I'm preparing for
having you hammer me
Back to my dingy corner
Of a loveless forever.

# Unfinished

You left me unfinished
In a way
You leave your paintings unfinished
As though no more could be done
As though it would embrace
Halfness
You left me unfinished
In a way
That I would not be able to find
Someone as valuable as you
To complete me,
Or the voids in my body.

# Absence of you

Not one minute goes by in the absence of you
In my numb health
Not one night can I spend
In spiritual solace
Letting go of the bag full of our moments,
That breaks my spine
All of my empty hours are filled with the thoughts of you
But empty still because of the absence of you
Emptiness would turn into nothingness and I'll not know what either one is
Because of the absence of you
I'll cry in pain,
I'll hunt for hints from you,
But what will I do about the absence of you?
And I'll divide myself in
Me and you
But I will figure out the absence of you.
And those nightmares will get friendly
They might even depress me more each passing day
For there won't be you to comfort me
But just
The absence of you.
I'll shut my doors
I'll shut my windows,
Lay in bed like a wilted rose
And all by myself, I will try to escape

The painful
Absence of you.
Walking those streets,
My legs would shake,
my voice would tremble and I'll cry again
For those streets and my side
Would suffer from the absence of you.
I said I'll wait forever
So that's what I'll do,
Till I am dead enough to not feel the absence of you.

# Futile

It's only August,
But I'm freezing
Because the core of me
Was so engaged in imploring
For your innocent attention,
That it forgot that one day,
It's going to be left,
Deserted.
Without the resources to warm me.
One day,
you are going to be ice cold
And to reach you
I would walk for miles
barefoot on ice,
I'll ask you to notice
How much I have suffered
To see you build a fireplace
With someone else.

# Very

I'll look at the blue sky through the browns of your
eyes.
And tell you how much I want to fix that sight to mine.
I'll see pieces of your hair dancing to the music of the
wind.
Your necklines and collar bone would explain that
you're nervous,
And your chest would be as though plains of the perfect
mountain
Your hips would hold the lives I am going to give,
And your feet would walk with me
Visit horizons
You'll go in and out of me,
Adjust the spaces of my body so that it fits you
perfectly,
Till we're drained out.
I'll rest my head into your bare chest,
And we'll feel our hearts at the same pace,
Breath coordinated,
Hands interlocked,
Eyes staring.
And I'll say
*We're so deep in love*
And you'd say
*Very.*

# Lilac

You come out in the evenings,
and make us blush - the sky and I.
We turn lilac in the warmth of your presence
that does not hunt
for either one of us.
Eventually because of which,
the sky and I
Go back to being blue,
till we're finished with
Filling the palette full of lilac
On our cheeks,
by the sight of you.

# Manipulative

Your love,
Manipulated nature for me.
It held so much priority.
The way you brought us heartbreak though,
Came to me like the sour taste of candies.
The way you turned cold overnight,
Made me palpitate.
You watched me panic,
Watched me break and so simply,
You turned away.
And I barely believe myself,
When I see the girl in the mirror
Ready.
To buckle up and grow.

# Hold me

Only hold me,
When I'm trembling
Walking through the place,
that holds our memories.
Only hold me,
when I feel so helpless
about touching your solid figure.
Only hold me,
When I cry to my starry skies,
Hopelessly expecting an interaction with you.
Only hold me,
When I start shivering, reliving your presence.
Only hold me,
Every second of my life
Until I don't feel this loss
So vehemently.

# Transparent skies

So when I looked up,
I saw no clouds
And the sky bare body hid nothing.
When I looked up I saw you again,
In it's exposed chest.
I know it's easier for me to spot you in the sky,
But it must be so difficult for you to find me in this world.
It must be so difficult for you to still see me trying to find love.
Love, I promise you my honesty,
I will never find someone as loving as you.
Just sit tight, I'm not taking forever, literally, to make it to you.
I know it'll take me seventy long years maybe a day
To leave my body to this world.
But don't you give up on yourself
Like you did when you were here.
I'm always going to look for you in my skies.
I can't handle being in the same place, same land where you lost so much courage.
So I'll dedicatedly lose mine and
Evaporate.
Collect me and my softly blown ashes
And put me together into a person,
Into someone you can love fearlessly.

# Lesions

How do I manage?
To make you care about
The lesions you have caused in me

# Tell me

Tell me why you quietly spread
Rubbles on my emotional future?
Tell me why you came in my life
Like poisoned chalice?
Tell me why you weakened
My diamond- protected heart,
That they're all shattered and mixed
With the rubbles you threw around?

# The premature wilting

Can you pause this music,
That sings of persuading me to move on.
I know what you wish for,
While you push me away,
While you keep showing my still figure,
The way out of your life.
I know that you're only
Growing a tree, in your garden
Where I once grew into a sunflower.
You're only depriving me of all the sun I need.
So that I choosingly wilt
And give up on being a part of your growth.
So that I give up on having my demands in your garden.
So that I don't have expectations.
And all other flowers witness
A premature wilting
Of a flower so full of nectar, full of only love.

# Elegant man

I feel for you so intense
That even your wilderness,
at times
Seemed like manly elegance.

# Prison

It's dimly lit,
The chambers of my heart,
Where the prisoners live.
Who have been plunged in affection and fruit.
Yet they cried for freedom and tasting humanity.
The prisoners
Have become so covetous,
After having lived on the golden of my body,
After walking on the cushion of
Thick experiences.
Who have always been
Suffering fulfilment.
They are prisoners
Of niceness beyond humanity
They are prisoners to love
Love from me.

## Cosmic aggression

The day you left,
The sun in my world died.

# Flashbacks

It happens very often
That I am blinded by our memories
Out of nowhere,
My stomach would hold snowstorms
And my head would go run back to when
You and I began to be.

# Caves

Take me to the cave
Of where your ripped soul lives
With only abandonment in it's company.
Take me to those moist walls
From the black rain
And ash grey skies.
I have seen you dipped in diamond
But I know you suffer,
From caped ghosts
That enter your soul, hungry,
In dark wilderness in search of a memory
That you have been wanting to forget.
Expose me to the
Darkest thoughts of yours.
Let it sprint through mine,
Let our tenebrosity have conversations,
About lighting scented candles in our caves.
Of where you and i now live
I call it a palace
That I have helped you make.
Even though the dust peeks through the golden walls.
It'll remain a mystery to the world,
When they see the paint from the walls,
Wearing off
And when it all reveals a cave
With relics of our unknown secrets smeared over our bones.

The world will ask the gatekeepers
Of whats and hows of our love,
And all they'll know is that
We let each other's secrets kill each other in the end.

# Cracked

Loneliness is a lot more
Than finding company in the cracks
Of the wall your bed is glued to.
The way I start crying
When I see cracks just anywhere
And feel as though you have caused it
Everywhere.
Because once upon a time
The world was home to me
And now it's cracked
Open into pitch darkness.
Now you're in my former home
Punching it, to expand.
Finding love, living in perfect trance.
But the punching is causing several other crack-births in my world.
Till it shrinks till it only fits my heart
And then you'll happily crack that too.

# Bee

You flew like a bee
Made me, a flower
Your transit.
You sipped on my nectar,
Till it was bitter and dry.
Beautifully,
We became symbiotic
And matched our yellows,
Became subject to tiny Polaroids.
So after, I fell in love
With a bee that could also cause me so much pain,
I promised you,
That I'll withhold the sweet.
But it's so silly of me,
To think
That I could be the tastiest flower
You'll ever transit.